MAYAN MYSTERY

Nick Hunter

Illustrated by
David Pavon

OXFORD
UNIVERSITY PRESS

CONTENTS

LOST CITIES OF THE MAYA

The steamy rainforests of Central America are the scene of one of history's greatest mysteries. Underneath the dense trees and vines lie the remains of a network of cities. These were once home to millions of people called the Maya. Their streets and houses have disappeared beneath the forest, and only their great stone pyramids and temples remain. The great mystery is: what happened to the Maya?

The Mayan civilization was made up of more than 30 **city-states**, spread across an area that is now Guatemala, Belize and southern Mexico. Each city was home to as many as 100 000 people, meaning they were some of the biggest cities on Earth at the time.

This is the area where the Maya built their civilization.

Mexico

Belize

Guatemala

Honduras

El Salvador

Nicaragua

DISASTER STRIKES

The Mayan culture reached its height around 250 CE and this **classic period** lasted for almost 700 years. But around 900 CE, something went badly wrong. Great Mayan cities seem to have been abandoned, to be reclaimed by the rainforest.

LOOKING FOR CLUES

Since archaeologists and scientists began to study Mayan ruins almost 200 years ago, they have been trying to solve the mystery of the dramatic end of the civilization. Did the Maya face a terrible natural disaster or a catastrophic famine? Were their cities destroyed by invaders or by fighting between the Maya themselves?

Like any good detective, we should start by looking at how the Maya lived: can their lives and culture give us clues about their fate?

SCIENCE

We can learn about the Maya from the carvings they left behind.

SCIENCE SOLUTIONS

New scientific discoveries have given us vital clues about the fate of the Maya. Scientists can find evidence in the skeletons of Maya people who died more than 1000 years ago. The latest techniques can also help us to explore the climate and rainfall on which the Mayan way of life depended.

DISCOVERING THE MAYA

Explorers, archaeologists and scientists have pored over the ruins of the Mayan civilization to try and unravel their secrets. But not all of their conclusions have been correct.

BURNING BOOKS

Bishop de Landa did huge damage to our knowledge of the Maya by burning books and destroying idols that depicted human **sacrifices**. Spanish troops murdered many Maya people who tried to stop him.

1566:

After the Spanish invasion of Mayan lands, Bishop Diego de Landa writes the first outsider's account of the Mayan civilization.

1787:

Spanish Captain Antonio del Rio explores the Mayan city of Palenque (say pa-len-kay), which local people had recently rediscovered. Del Rio concluded that the ruins showed Greeks or Romans had conquered the region. He did not believe that local people could have built the magnificent structures he found there.

1500   1600   1700   1800

Catherwood's beautiful images revealed the treasures of the Maya to the world.

1839 – 1842:

American John Lloyd Stephens and British artist Frederick Catherwood explore the ruins of Mayan civilization. Stephens and Catherwood were convinced that the buildings were not the work of visitors from another continent, but they had no way of knowing how old they were.

The Le Plongeons (say plaw-jawhn) pioneered the use of photography in archaeology, but their conclusions about the Maya's links to the Egyptian pyramids were wildly incorrect.

1870s:

Augustus and Alice Le Plongeon excavate the site of Chichen Itza (say chi-chen ee-tsa). They suggest the idea that the Mayan ruins had some link to ancient Egypt or even the lost land of **Atlantis**.

1881 – 1894:

British archaeologist Alfred Percival Maudslay explores the region, collecting statues and making moulds of carvings and inscriptions. Maudslay's work enabled others to study and finally decipher the Mayan calendar. They now knew when the Maya had lived.

2012:

Archaeologists uncover the oldest known Mayan calendar.

1900

2000

1946:

American Giles Healey discovers murals at Bonampak showing war and human sacrifice, which reveal the reality of war between Mayan city-states.

Present:

New discoveries are still being made which could change our understanding of these mysterious people or explain the riddle of the Mayan collapse.

"Here were the remains of a cultivated, polished and peculiar people, who had passed through all the stages ... of the rise and fall of nations, had reached their golden age, and had perished, entirely unknown."

John Lloyd Stephens describes what he and Catherwood found at Palenque

THE RISE OF THE MAYA

If you could travel back in a time machine almost 3000 years to the lush forests of Central America, you would find yourself in the first settlements of the great Mayan civilization. That civilization would go on to dominate the region for almost two **millennia**.

Around 800 BCE, the Maya spread out from the mountains of the Pacific coast, where they had lived for thousands of years. The search for better farmland to grow crops drew them to the central lowlands of Guatemala and southern Mexico, where they would live until their disappearance 1700 years later.

The thatched houses in the earliest Mayan villages would not look too different from the houses that many of the Maya's descendants still live in today. Gradually, these isolated villages became permanent settlements. Around 300 BCE, the Maya began to build the first temples and pyramids that would dominate their growing cities.

SLASH AND BURN

The Maya were farmers, living on a diet of maize, beans and chilli peppers. To grow these crops they had to clear areas of the dense jungle using simple stone axes and burning the undergrowth. The ash from this 'slash and burn' process enriched the soil so that they could grow crops.

The fields would only be fertile for a few years before the farmers had to clear a new area of jungle. But despite this exhausting and time-consuming work, over hundreds of years they began to build an advanced and cultured civilization.

ANCIENT CHOCOLATE

Did you know?

Early Maya settlers were the first people to turn the seeds of the cacao tree into chocolate. Archaeologists have discovered traces of a bitter chocolate drink on ancient pottery fragments.

This is a statue of the Mayan maize god. For many of the Maya, maize was almost their only food.

Olmec remains include giant carved heads up to three metres tall.

THE OLMEC

The Maya were not the first civilization in Central America. The Olmec built large towns in southern Mexico around 1500 BCE. Their language and culture had a big influence on the Maya.

But Olmec culture declined about 1100 years later, and archaeologists aren't sure why. They relied on a small number of food crops, so changes in climate could have led to disastrous food shortages, or the crops could have been destroyed by warfare between tribes.

THE CITY-STATES

If you adjust your time machine to take you to the Mayan lands around 100 BCE, you'll see a very different landscape. Many of the simple farming villages have now expanded to become large cities. Giant temples and pyramids tower above you.

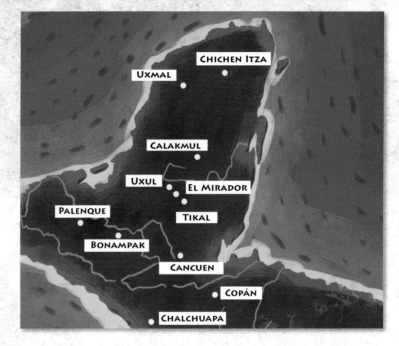

The structures of Mayan cities were closely linked to the natural world and religion. Pyramids represented the mountains to the south of the Mayan lands. The wide open spaces at the heart of the city were supposed to signify lakes.

El Mirador was the largest Mayan city at this time. The grand buildings at its centre were connected to the swampy farmland around it by a series of **causeways**. The city's central pyramid towered 70 metres into the air. Ceremonial buildings were adorned with figures from Mayan religion, such as a giant bird god.

Other majestic cities included Tikal, Copán and Palenque. As well as their dramatic architecture, these cities all boasted a well-developed writing system, a calendar, and great achievements in art and science. Their leaders were also fiercely independent and fought constant wars as city-states made and broke **alliances** with neighbouring rulers.

A Golden Age

From 250 CE, the Maya entered a golden age. Populations of the city-states grew steadily and traded with each other as well as with other cultures such as the great city of Teotihuacan (*say tay-o-ti-wa-kan*) in central Mexico.

The Maya enjoyed centuries of wealth and success. However, they did not enjoy peace, as battles between the cities continued to rage. Fierce competition for power and status meant that the most powerful city-states would rise or fall depending on their military successes. Often these fierce rivals lived just a few miles apart.

Understanding what Mayan society was like in this period may give us clues to why it came to an end.

SCIENCE

RADIOCARBON DATING

Radiocarbon dating is a powerful tool that scientists use to find the age of ancient remains. Natural materials such as wood and bone contain tiny traces of a particular type of carbon. This decays over time at a steady rate. By measuring the amount of carbon left, scientists can discover very accurately the age of an ancient skeleton or when a piece of wood was used in a building.

Carved wooden doors can be tested to reveal when they were created.

THE WORLD OF THE MAYA

We can enter the remarkable world of the Maya through the ruins that they left behind. By examining their buildings, art and carvings, archaeologists have been able to uncover a complex, cultured but also brutal civilization.

PLEASING THE GODS

The dramatic skylines of Mayan cities, with their pyramids and temples, were shaped by the Mayan religion. Religion was at the heart of Mayan society and their temples were full of religious paintings and sculptures.

BLOOD OFFERINGS

Bloody sacrifices were an essential feature of religious **rituals**, including the sacrifice of prisoners. The Maya also used a string threaded with thorns to cut their own cheeks, lips and tongues. They thought this would please the gods and help their crops to grow.

Did you know?

SACRED SPORT

For the Maya, sport really was a religion. Close to the temples in most cities was a ball court shaped like a capital I. Players competed to push the ball to either end of the court using their hips and without touching it with hands or feet. This game was probably part of a religious ritual. Winning mattered, as the penalty for losing could be death.

Murals found at Bonampak provided a clear picture of the warlike Maya.

ITZAMNA

The Maya worshipped a vast array of different gods. The most important was Itzamna, the creator god, who the Maya believed had taught them to write and to create their calendar. The god often appeared in four separate forms, linked to north, south, east and west. Itzamna was the **patron** of **scribes** and priests, the educated people of Mayan city-states.

TIME AND THE LONG COUNT

Time was incredibly important to the Maya. Their complicated calendar used a 365-day period similar to our own year as well as a 260-day period. These periods combined in the Long Count, which traced Mayan history from 3114 BCE in our modern calendar. This Long Count was used to mark births, events and the reigns of kings. It is by deciphering this count that archaeologists can trace the history of the Maya accurately, including the dates of their collapse.

Did you know?

MAYAN MATHS

The Maya were one of the earliest people to develop the idea of zero in maths. They wrote numbers as a series of dots and dashes. Mayan numbers were organized in groups of 20 instead of our decimal system which is based on groups of 10. The Mayan system was probably based on the number of human fingers and toes.

SYSTEM OF WRITING

One of the keys to unlocking the Maya's secrets was deciphering their system of writing. The code was finally cracked in the 1950s, and archaeologists could understand the writings and carvings of the Maya for the first time. Experts started to put together a picture of city-states led by warlords who battled against one another.

Numerous different languages were spoken across the Mayan city-states, but only two or three of these were ever written down. Maya scribes used hundreds of different glyphs, or images, arranged in blocks. Some of these glyphs depicted whole words, while others represented sounds or syllables.

To crack the Maya's code, archaeologists not only had to work out what the glyphs meant, but also which order to read them in.

Among the greatest treasures from the Mayan civilization are the few remaining books, or **codices**. These were long strips of bark folded together like fans, and only a few of them survived the book burning of Spanish invaders. These fragments contain vital details of Mayan religion and Maya priests' detailed understanding of the stars and planets.

A page from one of the few surviving Mayan codices.

Stelae (singular: stela) are stone columns covered with intricate carvings and markings, which are full of clues about Mayan life. The inscriptions tell the stories of the rulers of Mayan city-states, celebrating their reigns and their victories. The largest stelae could weigh up to 10 tonnes.

ONLY THE STRONG SURVIVE

In 1952, Mexican archaeologist Alberto Ruz Lhuillier (*say* le-hu-lee-ay) was investigating a temple at Palenque when he noticed a slab in the floor with a row of holes. They looked like finger holes. After lifting the slab, Lhuillier and his team found a long, narrow staircase leading down into the darkness. At the bottom was a vast stone chamber containing a tomb. Inside was a body, buried with fabulous treasures and covered in precious **jade** jewellery.

The tomb of Pacal lies beneath the imposing Temple of the Inscriptions.

A ROYAL DISCOVERY

The tomb had been built for King Pacal the Great, who ruled Palenque from 615 to 684 CE and made it one of the most powerful city-states. The discovery was important because it showed that the great stone pyramids of the Maya were built to honour dead rulers as well as for religious rituals.

Did you know?

ANCIENT ASTRONAUT

Pacal's **sarcophagus** is decorated with an image of the king that has led to some outrageous theories. Could it show King Pacal at the controls of a spacecraft? This idea has been put forward by supporters of the theory that the Maya were contacted by visitors from another planet. Experts believe that the image actually shows the king on his journey to the afterlife.

King Pacal the Great's jade death mask.

TOMB TECHNOLOGY

In 2011, archaeologists used a small remote-controlled camera to explore a tomb at Palenque. The tomb was beneath a pyramid that could have collapsed if archaeologists had ventured into it themselves. Investigators believed the tomb might be the last resting place of an early queen of Palenque, one of the few known female rulers.

BETWEEN HEAVEN AND EARTH

The throne of a Mayan city-state was usually passed down from father to son. Pacal was unusual as he inherited the throne from his mother. Rulers were **revered** by their people, who saw them as the link between heaven and earth. Their elaborate dress and public rituals demonstrated that these leaders were different and special. Pacal's lavish tomb shows that, in good times, kings could amass great wealth.

The power of the Mayan civilization was determined by the strength of its kings. Each of around 60 city-states had its own ruler. They made alliances and fought wars against their rival states. But a king was only as strong as his last victory, and if he lost a battle, the unfortunate ruler might find himself being sacrificed by his conqueror.

SOCIAL ORDER

Mayan society was rigidly organized. The noble classes were made up of the leader's family, government officials, priests, high-ranking warriors and merchants. Scribes, who knew the complex code of Mayan glyphs, were usually members of noble families. Ordinary families were each given a plot of land to farm, with a proportion of their crops being paid as taxes. Many of those working on the land were slaves who had been captured in battle or traded between the states.

The Maya did not have precious metals such as gold and silver. Jewellery made from green jade was the ultimate status symbol for rich Maya.

HANGING ON TO POWER

The position of the king, and the order of society, rested on two things: prosperity and military power. The Maya believed that everything was planned by the gods. If the rains did not come one year and the harvest failed, the gods must be unhappy. This was also true if they allowed the king to be defeated in battle.

Battles could be brutal. The Maya fought with spears and clubs covered with sharp stone blades. There was no mercy for the losers. Kings and leaders would be executed. Ordinary soldiers would spend the rest of their lives as slaves.

Mayan cities did not always fight alone. The children of ruling families were often married to each other in order to build alliances between states. Two of the greatest rivals were Tikal and Calakmul. They each allied with smaller states to build their military might.

Warriors wore cotton body armour that had been soaked in saltwater. This made it surprisingly tough.

Did you know?

DEFENDING THE CITY

Most Mayan cities did not have walls to protect them from attack, until some built defences in a hurry at the time of the Mayan collapse. Who or what were they afraid of?

In spite of the destructive wars between their rulers, Mayan states did not stop trading with each other. They continued to put up elaborate buildings, and the population grew. However, after 750 CE, things began to change. This was the start of the Mayan collapse, but what did it look like and how do we know about it?

DECLINE AND FALL

The greatest years of the Mayan civilization were in the 8th century CE. Grand buildings adorned the growing cities as the Maya population continued to increase. Maya priests studied the stars and other signs, believing that they could predict the future, but could they have foreseen what would have happened to their civilization by 900 CE?

The great change that we call the Mayan collapse did not happen in a single day or even a single year. In the late 700s, old alliances between city-states crumbled and trading links between them started to break down. There had always been conflict, but now it grew fiercer as rulers tried to seize more land as well as fighting for the glory that came with victory.

ABANDONED CITIES

Disaster struck different city-states in different ways. For many, the end was quick and violent as they were destroyed by invading armies or possibly in an uprising of their own people. Elsewhere, the reasons for a city-state's decline are much less clear.

What archaeologists are certain of is that after 800 CE many of the cities that had thrived for hundreds of years were abandoned, right across the lowland areas that had been the heart of the classic Mayan civilization.

DESTRUCTION OF CANCUEN

Archaeologists have been able to piece together the details of a devastating attack on the city of Cancuen (*say* kan-koon) in 800 CE. The attackers swept into the city, leaving a trail of destruction. Monuments and statues were destroyed or left unfinished.

The attackers executed the king and several noble prisoners. The city was never rebuilt and we know nothing about the attackers or why they attacked. They were not interested in stealing the fine jewellery, which they left with their victims.

This panel celebrates the ruler of Cancuen.

PROTECTING THE EVIDENCE

The evidence that could explain the fate of the Maya is spread across hundreds of different sites in the jungles of Central America. No one could visit all of these sites and archaeologists spend years uncovering the secrets of a single site such as Cancuen. Over hundreds of years, much of the evidence has been destroyed by the passing of time or sometimes deliberately. Mayan ruins are still under threat as the forest is cleared to build new roads and towns. The quest to explain the Mayan collapse is a race against time.

SIGNPOSTS FOR DISASTER

Much of what we know about the Mayan collapse comes from things that stopped happening. After 800 CE, many cities stopped erecting stelae, the stone columns that had been used for centuries to mark the reigns of kings. There were no new building projects after 830 CE, and few examples of Mayan writing from after this date have been discovered.

Across the region palaces were abandoned. The Maya's strict social order broke down as other people built their homes inside these crumbling ruins. Finally, the cities seem to have been totally abandoned. Within a century, a population of several million people had almost completely disappeared.

Around 1500 years ago, these ruins in the jungle would have been the heart of a great city.

SCIENCE

POPULATION PROBLEM

The United States National Aeronautical and Space Administration (NASA) is most famous for launching astronauts into space, but NASA scientists have used satellite data and advances in science to study the Mayan remains. They calculated that, by 800 CE, the Mayan lands had one of the densest populations of the ancient world. Mayan cities were home to more people per square kilometre than many modern cities. All the food for these people had to be grown on the land around the cities.

NASA investigators hope that by explaining the reasons for the Mayan collapse, they can prevent a similar catastrophe in future.

The Maya developed sophisticated farming techniques, but changes in soil and climate were constant challenges, as they still are today.

SOLVING THE MYSTERY

Archaeologists are certain that something dramatic happened to the Maya after 800 CE. The remains show a dramatic reduction in population, but written records do not help us to find the reasons for this.

The question we need to answer is why the Mayan collapse happened. The Maya tried to live in harmony with nature, to grow their crops in the thin soil and difficult climate of the homelands. Did this relationship with nature break down, or was the Mayan collapse caused by the Maya themselves?

THE FINAL COUNTDOWN

We are able to pinpoint the dates of the Mayan collapse very accurately because of their obsession with dates. Events in Mayan history were always recorded, up to the point where the records stopped.

Archaeologists who have spent their lives studying the Maya are still not sure what happened, but over the next few chapters we will look at some of their theories, from the convincing to the crazy. Then you can decide for yourself what became of the Maya.

THEORY 1: NATURAL DISASTER

Mayan myths about the creation of the world included a figure called Earthquake, who could make mountains fall to the ground by tapping his foot. This is just one story that shows the close connection between the Maya and the land they lived on. Their supply of food was totally dependent on the soil and the rain that watered their crops. Nature sustained the Mayan cities, but could it also have destroyed them?

FORCES OF NATURE

The region has been battered by nature's strongest forces since long before the age of the Maya, and the threat continues.

EARTHQUAKES

Earthquakes can cause terrible damage – in 1985, a powerful earthquake that hit the area around Mexico City killed at least 10 000 people. Some Mayan buildings were certainly ruined by powerful tremors. However, there is no sign of a quake which could have threatened the entire civilization.

HURRICANES

Fierce hurricanes are also a regular hazard in the region. These violent storms could destroy crops and damage buildings. It might have taken time for the Maya to recover, but a hurricane would not have had a huge and lasting impact.

Hurricanes are still a threat to the lives and homes of Central America's people.

VOLCANOES

The Maya lived in the shadow of several active volcanoes. Pyramids in cities close to the mountains were often built to have fires on top of them, to mimic the smoking peaks. The volcanoes provided fertile volcanic soil, but there was also the risk of a devastating eruption.

The Mayan village of Chalchuapa (*say* kal-chi-wa-pa) was buried by ash from a nearby volcano around 400 CE and there was a major eruption of the volcano Popocatepetl (*say* po-po-kat-a-pe-tal) around 800 CE. Scientists have found evidence of volcanic ash and heat damage in the ruins of Palenque, one of the first cities to be abandoned.

VOLCANIC VALUE

Scientists believe volcanoes were actually a good thing for the Maya. Volcanic ash was carried by the wind across the less fertile land in lowland areas, making the thin soil more suited to growing crops.

Mount Popocatepetl towers over central Mexico and is one of the region's most active volcanoes.

NO EASY ANSWERS

A dramatic natural disaster seems like a simple solution to the Mayan mystery, but unfortunately it is far too neat. The Mayan collapse happened very quickly by historical standards, but it probably took several decades. These cities were not all destroyed or abandoned overnight because of some dramatic disaster. It is possible that a major volcanic eruption, throwing millions of tonnes of ash into the atmosphere, could have disrupted normal weather patterns, causing a series of bad harvests across the region.

The Maya believed that disease and disaster came from the gods, who could be calmed with bloodletting.

EPIDEMIC

Not all natural disasters happen as suddenly and destructively as an earthquake. The cities seem to have been abandoned rather than destroyed. What could have happened to the millions of people who lived in them?

One explanation is that the Maya were hit by a terrible disease. We know that when European invaders arrived in Mexico in the 1500s, they brought diseases such as smallpox that were totally new to the Americas. These diseases wiped out almost all of the native people, who had no natural defence against them. The hot, humid conditions were perfect breeding grounds for bugs and parasites. The Maya did not have the medical knowledge to deal with a disease spreading rapidly through the population.

RESISTING DISEASE

The immune system is the body's way of resisting disease. The immune system develops cells that attack disease-causing **micro-organisms**. If a new disease attacked the Maya population, their immune system might not have been able to defend against it. The poor diet of some Maya people would also have made their bodies weaker and more vulnerable to an epidemic.

For most of history, humans (including the Maya) had no idea that diseases were spread by micro-organisms such as these smallpox bacteria. They had no effective way to stop an epidemic from spreading.

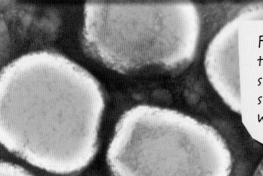

For and Against

Was the Mayan collapse caused by a natural disaster?

For
- Area regularly affected by earthquakes, volcanic eruptions, hurricanes.
- We know of at least two Mayan settlements buried by volcanic ash; some scientists believe Palenque suffered something similar.
- Millions of people were wiped out by disease in later centuries when the Spanish invaded. Maybe this also happened before.

Against
- Mayan collapse did not happen overnight, ruling out the possibility of a sudden natural disaster across the whole region.
- No evidence of a catastrophic earthquake at this time.
- If the Maya were hit by an epidemic, why is there no written record of it?

THEORY 2: ENVIRONMENTAL CHANGE

Today, the lands where Mayan farmland and cities once stood are almost totally covered with dense rainforest. It is hard to imagine how different the land would have looked 1200 years ago. Around 800 CE, there were several million Maya living in the region that is now covered by this forest. Cities would have been surrounded not by forest but by farmland as far as the eye could see. Complex irrigation systems

channelled water from rivers and lakes. Without this water, the crops would fail and millions of Maya would face drought and famine.

DEFORESTATION

To create this farmland, the Maya must have cleared vast numbers of trees. This process is known as deforestation. In the early days of the Maya, farmers only used an area of land for a few years before moving on and allowing the poor soil to recover. However, the growing population meant that any suitable land was already occupied. They had no choice but to keep using the same land to grow crops. Even though the Maya had invented sophisticated irrigation and farming systems, the nutrients in the ground would eventually be exhausted and the harvests would get poorer and poorer. This could not continue forever. Either the people would have to find new land or they would face starvation.

Scientists have used **computer models** to calculate that, if all the forests in the region were removed, the local temperature would rise by several degrees. Sunlight that is currently reflected by the canopy of trees would warm the ground. This would evaporate more water and make it more difficult to grow crops.

POLLEN POSER

Analysing sediment in the beds of lakes can reveal secrets about changes in the environment 1200 years ago. Scientists have discovered that, at the time of the collapse, almost no tree pollen was being produced in the region. This supports the theory that the area had been cleared of forest at this time.

> There were tens of millions of people in the area, and they were building cities and farms at the expense of the forest.
>
> **Climate scientist Benjamin Cook,**
> *National Geographic*, November 2012

DROUGHT

The biggest danger if temperatures did rise was that this would lead to a disruption of the normal weather patterns, particularly essential rainfall. New research methods enable us to get an idea of how climates have changed over time, and many experts are convinced that the Mayan lands suffered a catastrophic drought around the time of the Mayan collapse.

Drought would have caused bad harvests, leading to insufficient food for the growing population. Just as importantly, drinking water would have been affected. Some Mayan states were not close to a river. They relied on storing water in reservoirs. A dry reservoir would spell disaster for thousands of people.

Drought itself would have led to deaths from hunger and thirst. Lack of food and water would have struck at the very basis of Mayan society. This, in turn, would have led to other consequences. People who are hungry are much more likely to wage war on their neighbours for precious resources. And people who are hungry are much more likely to question the people who lead their society and to rise up against them.

Drought was not just a problem for the Maya. Millions of people today live with the threat of famine if the year's expected rain does not fall.

For and Against

Did the Maya face environmental disaster?

For
- Archaeological evidence shows that the Maya population had reached record levels; overpopulation put an extra strain on farmland.
- Scientists have used computer models and concluded deforestation could lead to a warmer climate and reduced rainfall.
- Stalagmite and lake bed research shows evidence of major drought.

Against
- No indication from stelae and other sources that society was facing drought.
- Some cities were close to rivers, so would have been less affected. They had sophisticated farming methods to deal with drought.
- Cities on the edge of Mayan lowlands do not seem to have been affected.

SCIENCE

DROUGHT DISCOVERY

Stalagmites are formed by mineral deposits that have dripped from the roofs of caves. Scientists can run tests on stalagmites in order to find out how much rain fell in the distant past. Using this technique, researchers have concluded that the region suffered 80 years of very dry conditions around the time of the Mayan collapse.

THEORY 3: CLASS CONFLICT

The pyramids and palaces at the heart of Mayan cities show us that status mattered to the Maya. But the strict class system that organized their society may also be the key to understanding their civilization's destruction.

THE CLASS SYSTEM

The kings of Mayan city-states were at the top of the class system. They were revered by their people, who built them vast palaces and ornate tombs. Stelae praised the exploits of these great leaders. The ordinary Maya knew their own place in society as workers for the leader.

As the city-states grew richer and more powerful, more and more people came to depend directly on the leader. Members of the growing royal families probably took the important jobs as military generals and government officials. The leader also had to show his power by staging lavish religious rituals and ordering great building projects. During the 700s, kings competed to build more impressive monuments than their neighbours.

Dancers, cooks, artists, scribes and many more people were needed to keep this royal show going. These officials and palace workers, living in the **opulent** hearts of the cities, became increasingly distant from the Maya out in the fields who grew their food and built their temples.

Noble families distinguished themselves in many ways, including their ornate dress and headdresses. Their jewellery was made from exotic jade.

Maya leaders used huge buildings and lavish ceremonies to show off their power and wealth.

Did you know?

TAX COLLECTORS

The nobles sent tax collectors to collect some of each farmer's crop. As crop failure became more regular and demands for taxes grew, these tax collectors must have become very unpopular.

CHANGES IN SOCIETY

The nobles' demand for luxuries such as jade jewellery and feathers of the prized quetzal bird probably led the ordinary people to resent their leaders, especially in times of drought and climate change. Food was getting scarce and their powerful rulers were not doing much about it. Did these changes lead to revolutions across the Mayan civilization, with the ruling classes being murdered by their hungry people?

THE EVIDENCE

The idea of the downtrodden Maya rising up against their mighty leaders is a great story, but is there any evidence to support it? Archaeologists have to work like detectives, piecing together often gruesome details to try and solve an ancient crime.

In 2013, investigators in the Mayan city of Uxul (*say* oosh-ool) made a horrifying discovery. They found the bodies of 24 murdered Maya. The slivers of precious jade inlaid in the teeth of some victims suggested they may have been nobles, but when their skeletons were studied, others showed signs of the bad diet eaten by many ordinary Maya.

A few years before the massacre at Uxul, wealthy people had been targeted in the attack on Cancuen. Many of the city's carvings and monuments were also deliberately destroyed.

Were they killed by poorer Maya enraged by hunger and thirst, or were they simply prisoners or victims of a war between city-states? We may never know, but our knowledge of the Maya is improving with each new discovery, as advanced scientific techniques help us to find out more about how ancient people lived and died.

SCIENCE

CSI CANCUEN

The bodies discovered at Cancuen had been well preserved for hundreds of years. Investigators could tell from the wounds on the victims that they had been executed and not killed in battle.

Did you know

UNWRITTEN STORIES

Experts believe that fewer than one in four Maya could read and write. If the kings, nobles and their scribes were forced from power, that could explain the sudden end of Mayan written records.

Most ordinary people would not have understood the complex Mayan writing system.

For and Against

Did the Mayan civilization end due to revolution?

For
- Climate change and drought put huge pressure on harvests.
- Rigid system of social classes meant that ordinary Maya had no say in how their city-state was run — there was tension when things went badly.
- Graves of murdered nobles have been found, but the murderers are unknown.

Against
- Maya were not just one society but lots of city-states. Some may have been threatened by unrest, but not all.
- Some bodies found at Uxul were not nobles.
- Lack of clear evidence in writing or art.

THEORY 4: WAR

DISCOVERY AT BONAMPAK

In 1946, American archaeologist Giles Healey made an amazing discovery. Local people led him to a Mayan settlement called Bonampak that no outsider had visited before. What he found turned archaeologists' ideas about the Maya on their heads.

MURAL PAINTINGS

Healey found a series of breathtaking murals adorning the walls of three rooms within the ruins. The murals celebrated Bonampak's victory in a battle over a neighbouring state. The paintings did not just show the battle; they also showed the horrific way that the victors treated their prisoners, and particularly a figure who was probably the king of the defeated enemy. These bloody scenes were made worse by the contrasting scenes of music, dancing and partying in the background. The people of Bonampak were joyous about the death and destruction they had caused.

This reconstructed mural shows warriors attacking a Mayan village.

CLUES FROM ART

While the details of the paintings were shocking in themselves, their effect on our knowledge of the Maya was dramatic. Before this discovery, most archaeologists believed that the Maya lived relatively peaceful lives. There was one other important detail: the paintings were never completed. It is likely that the king who ordered the paintings and the skilled artists who created them were forced to abandon their work, possibly due to a revenge attack for the terrible events shown in the murals. The victory they marked certainly did not last – within a few years the city was abandoned.

DESPERATE BATTLES

The paintings were created around 800 CE. We know that war was a regular event for the Maya, but about this time warfare was changing. Wars had previously been about status and displays of power, ending with the capture of the defeated king and high-ranking warriors. City-states were not normally invaded. Around 800 CE, wars became desperate struggles to control land and capture slaves.

SCIENCE

RECONSTRUCTING BONAMPAK

Archaeologists used new technology to explore every detail of the Bonampak murals. They photographed the images using infrared light, which revealed previously invisible details and also showed how the murals were painted. Artists then recreated the paintings using Mayan techniques and materials.

EXPERT THEORIES

Experts have two possible theories about why violence between city-states spun out of control.

It could have been caused by fierce rivalry that had built up between states. They competed to build the biggest temples and to hold lavish festivals, and military competition also grew fiercer. But is it really possible that these battles grew so destructive that the Maya destroyed their own civilization?

The other possibility is that drought or climate change made the Maya desperate. War was no longer just about status. It was now about survival. The Maya attacked their neighbours to take their land, food and water.

INVASION

The chaos that broke out in the Mayan cities may not have been the fault of the Maya themselves. The powerful city-state of Teotihuacan in Mexico was overrun by invaders from the north of Mexico. Invaders could also have swept through the Mayan city-states, especially if the Maya were weakened by internal warfare or environmental change.

However, if foreign invaders had come to the Mayan lands, why would they have immediately abandoned the lands they conquered? They would probably have left some clear signs of their invasion. As it is, only a few paintings in isolated areas show warriors who were not wearing the usual Mayan dress. These invaders probably arrived after the disaster had started to overtake the Maya.

Maya generals went into battle dressed in fine clothes and wearing elaborate headdresses.

ARCHAEOLOGY UNDER FIRE

History detectives investigating the wars of the Maya are often hampered in their progress by present-day wars. Guatemala suffered from many years of civil war before a peace treaty in the 1990s. As well as destroying evidence, conflicts like this stop archaeologists from working safely. Criminal gangs also pose a danger to excavations in some areas, as they try to steal ancient artefacts to sell them for profit.

The figure on this stela looks different from other Maya warriors, and may have been an invader from outside the Mayan lands.

For and Against

Were the Maya destroyed by war or invasion?

For
- Archaeologists believe that wars grew more frequent and destructive at the time of the Mayan collapse.
- Cities such as Bonampak were abandoned and there is evidence of war in that region.
- Signs of outside influence in some states.

Against
- If war alone had caused the Mayan collapse, surely some of the more powerful states would have survived.
- Not much evidence of outside invasion across the whole region at this time.

THEORY 5: A MOVE TO THE COAST

All of the theories we have considered so far assume that the Maya who lived in the lowland cities were wiped out by a terrible catastrophe. There is plenty of evidence showing that they faced big challenges from conflict and the environment. But maybe the explanation is a bit simpler. Maybe the Maya just moved.

For hundreds of years before the Mayan collapse, the centre of Mayan civilization had been in lowland areas where cities such as Tikal and Palenque had grown rich and powerful. After the mysterious Mayan collapse, these cities were abandoned, but this did not happen everywhere in the Mayan world.

A NEW GOLDEN AGE?

Just as the pyramids and temples of the lowland cities were crumbling, other Mayan strongholds were enjoying the most glorious times in their history. Uxmal (*say* oosh-mal), Chichen Itza and cities close to the coast of the Gulf of Mexico enjoyed many years of success after the Mayan collapse in the central lowlands.

The Maya of the lowlands were traders as well as warriors. At the height of their power, the lowland region was criss-crossed with trade routes linking the cities to one another. They traded valuable goods such as cacao, jade and quetzal bird feathers. By the time of the Mayan collapse, trading along the coast became more important, bypassing the inland cities. If Maya merchants wanted to prosper, they had to move to the new trading cities. In addition, Maya farmers may have moved to the coast to escape the drought and warfare that were destroying the inland states.

Today, traditional canoes can still be seen in the Mayan lands.

Did you know?

CANOE TRADERS

We know that the Maya had no carts or other wheeled vehicles. Some Mayan cities were built along rivers that they used for trading by canoe. We cannot be sure why some cities, such as Tikal, were built far from rivers, where water was scarce in dry seasons. The sites may have had some religious significance.

WHY DID THE MAYA NEVER RETURN TO THEIR LOWLAND CITIES?

Archaeologists believe that cities such as Uxmal and Chichen Itza, which were closer to the Gulf of Mexico, did grow in the years after the Mayan collapse. This could be because many Maya moved there from the central lowlands. However, although Chichen Itza continued to prosper, within a few generations most of the other northern cities were virtually abandoned. Drought and climate change may have been at the root of this decline too.

If the Maya did move to the coast, why did they never return to their former homes? The simplest explanation is that life was easier in the northern cities along the coast, even if the climate had changed. Their diet could include more fish, which meant they did not have to rely so much on regular rainfall in order to grow crops and stay alive.

The Mayan city-states of the central lowlands may simply have been forgotten as new generations adapted to their new life. The old cities would have been swallowed up by trees and vegetation within a few years.

A QUESTION OF CULTURE

If this theory is correct, one mystery remains. What happened to the Maya's culture? No more stelae were built, and all sorts of myths, religious rituals and knowledge disappeared. This knowledge was controlled by the priests and scribes who were such an important part of the ruling class of the Mayan city-states. Could it be that these educated Maya did not survive to move to a new home? If so, maybe these high-ranking people were overthrown in a series of revolutions.

For and Against

Did the Maya move to new cities near the coast?

For
- Mayan cities near the sea saw growing populations and prosperity in the years after the Mayan collapse.
- Trade routes changed so there was less trade through the Maya's traditional lands.

Against
- What happened to the many aspects of Mayan culture that were lost after the collapse?
- Migration does not explain why Mayan cities were abandoned so quickly.

THEORY 6: ALIEN ABDUCTION

Some people are not convinced by the evidence gathered by archaeologists and scientists about the Mayan collapse. These people look at the mysterious ruins of Mayan temples and suspect something more mysterious than war or climate change: aliens.

There have been many claims of links between the Maya and **extraterrestrial** beings. Just as the early European explorers believed that Greeks and Romans built the Mayan pyramids, more recent doubters have stated that these great monuments were built by alien architects. Did these extraterrestrial visitors **abduct** the Maya and leave our planet forever? Or possibly their spacecraft are still hidden beneath the pyramids they built, as some people claim?

ASTRONOMY

Studying the night sky was a central part of Mayan culture. Maya priests were known as Servants of the Sun, and their main job was to mark time through the calendar and movements of the stars and planets across the sky. They also built **observatories** to study the skies. The movement of the planet Venus had an important bearing on Mayan religious beliefs.

This observatory at Chichen Itza enabled Maya **astronomers** to accurately plot the path of the planet Venus. Observatories have also been found in other Mayan cities.

EVIDENCE OF EXTRATERRESTRIALS

In 2011 it was claimed that the Mexican government had found proof of contact between the Maya and visitors from another planet. Pictures began to appear on blogs and websites showing a series of discs marked with images that were said to represent Earth seen from space, and an alien astronaut piloting a spacecraft. These images were supposedly created by the Maya or visiting alien artists.

Some people think that the Maya built pyramids as launch and landing sites for alien spacecraft.

 Did you know?

CONSPIRACY THEORY

Those who believe that extraterrestrial beings have visited Earth claim that governments have deliberately hidden evidence to keep this secret.

" Mexico will release codices, artefacts and significant documents with evidence of Maya and extraterrestrial contact, and all of their information will be **corroborated** by archaeologists. "

Documentary producer Raul Julia-Levy claimed that he had proof of extraterrestrial contact. But he never produced the evidence and Mayan experts remain unconvinced.

COULD IT BE TRUE?

The first problem is to decide whether visitors from another planet really exist. According to some sensational studies, more than 3 million Americans claim to have been abducted by aliens. Most scientists point out that there is no 'objective physical evidence' that could prove the existence of alien life.

So far, science has found no solid evidence of even the simplest microscopic life on other planets.

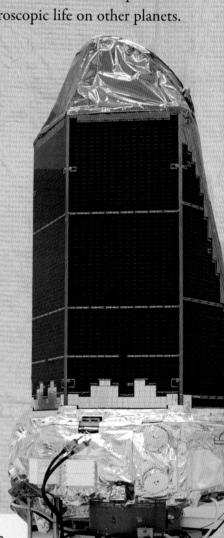

Astronomers using the Kepler telescope have discovered hundreds of Earth-like planets that could support life, but these planets are hundreds of light years away from Earth. If aliens did visit the Maya, they must have travelled a vast distance.

The images that are claimed as the main evidence for this theory have not been officially examined to prove that they are Mayan artefacts. Although blogs and websites claim the Mexican government released the discs, there has been no official comment about them.

The Kepler telescope scans the Universe for planets that could support life.

FACT OR FICTION

It can sometimes be difficult to work out if evidence for a theory is real. Detectives have to find ways of getting at the facts. Ask yourself these questions:

❖ Does the information come from a reliable source? Just because someone writes something on a website, that does not mean it is true. Official websites, such as those produced by the government or respected news organizations, are usually more reliable than a personal blog.

❖ If someone claims a picture was created by the Maya, do they have proof? Scientists have sophisticated ways to tell the age of an object or document.

❖ Is the source biased? If the evidence is supported by an archaeologist with no previous belief in alien life, that might make it more believable.

❖ Are there other ways of interpreting the information? You should always question new information that seems to contradict what you already know, but remember: many proven scientific ideas were once seen as strange or impossible!

For and Against
Were the Maya abducted by aliens?

For
- Many websites support the theory.
- The Maya had an amazing understanding of space.

Against
- None of the evidence gathered by scientists and archaeologists supports this theory.
- Pictures that claim to show evidence have not been officially verified.
- Currently there is no evidence of intelligent extraterrestrial life anywhere.

WHAT DO YOU THINK?

The mysterious collapse of the Mayan civilization is not a simple problem to solve. It happened over more than a century, in many different locations, and it affected millions of people. The specific reasons why each Mayan city was abandoned could be slightly different in each case.

Now that you have read the different theories about what happened to the Maya, make up your own mind about this historical puzzle.

Start by thinking about the different theories in turn. Ask yourself the following questions about each theory.

- What is the scientific and historical evidence for this theory? Ideas are more likely to be correct if they are based on hard evidence, such as archaeological and historical remains.

- Is the idea based on more than one piece of evidence? The more studies and physical objects there are to support an idea, the more convincing it is likely to be.

- What is the evidence against each theory? What arguments would you use if you were trying to disprove a particular explanation?

- Are the conclusions that have been drawn from the evidence convincing? For example, is it more likely that the pyramids and temples of the Mayan cities were built by the Maya themselves, or by aliens?

Remember, the answer to this mystery could be a combination of different factors. For example, changing climate and drought could have driven the Maya to revolution or caused warfare between them.

Even simple discoveries such as pottery fragments can help us to piece together how and when people lived in a place.

FACT AND OPINION

When evaluating the evidence for your theory, make sure you do not confuse facts and opinions:

❖ Facts are things that can be proved to have existed or happened. We can prove when and where the Maya lived because of historical remains such as pyramids and carved stelae marked with dates.

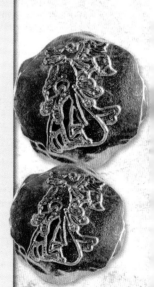

❖ Opinions can be based on known facts but they cannot be proved beyond doubt. We do not have any clear evidence to prove that the ordinary Maya overthrew their leaders, but some of the facts we know support the opinion that this could have happened.

To be a useful theory, an opinion needs to be backed up with facts and evidence.

THE MAYA TODAY

The Mayan collapse was the end of a remarkable civilization that had endured for centuries. Its cities were abandoned and much of its knowledge lost. But the Mayan collapse did not mean the end of the Maya as a people. Today there are around five million Maya, speaking 70 different languages, living in southern Mexico, Guatemala and Belize. What would you find if you visited the Maya today?

CLOSE TO NATURE

Despite conquests and disasters, the Maya still live in the same region of Central America where they have lived for millennia. This has helped them to keep their ancestors' strong connection to the natural world, although Mayan culture has been threatened by invaders and the influence of the modern world. Many Maya still wear traditional clothes and practise crafts that have been handed down over the centuries.

SPANISH INVADERS

In the early 1500s, the surviving Mayan cities and villages were conquered by Spanish invaders. The Maya suffered terrible epidemics and brutal treatment from their new masters. They were forced to convert to Christianity and lost many aspects of their own culture. Since Mexico and Guatemala gained independence from Spain, the Maya have often come into conflict with other population groups as they have tried to keep their distinctive culture.

DEADLY DISEASES

The Spanish invaders brought foreign diseases, such as measles and influenza, which killed 90 per cent of the native people, including the Maya.

THE LACANDON

Some Maya groups have become part of the Spanish-speaking population of the region. Others have struggled to remain separate. The Lacandon live in a few villages deep in the rainforest, where the mighty cities of the Maya once stood. They probably fled to their current home to escape Spanish invaders. Although there are only a few hundred Lacandon, they are very important to Mayan experts. They are the closest living culture to the ancient Maya; some even follow a version of the ancient religion.

"[Mayan civilization] didn't cease to exist; there are still today Maya people in the area. The culture, the traditions have been maintained."

Professor B. L. Turner, Arizona State University

MAYA UNDER THREAT

Like their ancient ancestors, today's Maya face many challenges to their culture and way of life. The forests of the ancient Mayan lands are now home to many Maya peasants who have been forced to move south from their own homelands in the highlands. Maya communities have often been persecuted by governments, or forced to move because of industry and tourism.

The few hundred Lacandon survive by hunting and growing food deep in the rainforest. In recent decades, their land has been threatened by timber companies cutting down the forest for its wood. Large areas of the forest have also been cleared for cattle farms, supplying beef to fast-food restaurants around the world.

FIGHTING BACK

Recently, there have been more attempts to protect Mayan culture, and Maya priests have been allowed to perform rituals at shrines in ancient cities such as Tikal. Schools in Guatemala even teach Maya pupils in their own language. After a struggle for survival that has continued since the time of the Mayan collapse, the Maya population is actually increasing.

The Maya have survived many challenges, and now they have a growing sense of their glorious past. As they battle against a changing environment and outside pressures on their culture, they probably have a real sense of the struggles their ancestors faced during the Mayan collapse. It remains to be seen whether this proud and distinctive culture will survive exposure to the modern world.

THE MAYAN CALENDAR

The Mayan calendar is still used today. Maya communities often have a priest whose job is to keep track of the complex system of dates and perform traditional Mayan rituals. On 21st December 2012, 5126 years of the Mayan Long Count came to an end and a new era of Mayan history began.

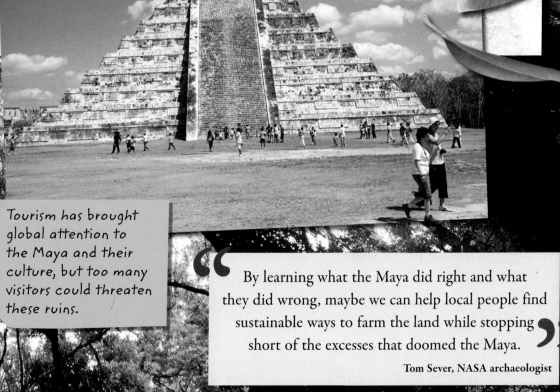

Tourism has brought global attention to the Maya and their culture, but too many visitors could threaten these ruins.

" By learning what the Maya did right and what they did wrong, maybe we can help local people find sustainable ways to farm the land while stopping short of the excesses that doomed the Maya. "

Tom Sever, NASA archaeologist

GLOSSARY

abduct: kidnap or capture someone against their will

alliances: agreements between two or more people or countries to help each other, for example in a war

astronomers: people who study objects in space, including stars and planets

Atlantis: mythical island civilization, first mentioned by ancient Greek philosopher Plato, which is supposed to have sunk into the Atlantic Ocean

causeways: raised paths or roads across a marshy or wet area

city-states: independent states with their own government, made up of a city and the surrounding land

classic period: the period when the Mayan civilization was at its most developed and successful, from about 250 to 900 CE

codices (singular: codex): ancient manuscripts or books

computer models: computer programs designed to show what happened or will happen in the future depending on certain factors, such as changes in climate

corroborated: confirmed or given support

extraterrestrial: from outside Earth or its atmosphere

jade: green precious stone highly prized by the Maya and used to make jewellery

micro-organisms: tiny creatures that are only visible through a microscope, such as bacteria or viruses

millennia (singular: millennium): periods of 1000 years, or ten centuries

observatories: buildings constructed for astronomers to study the stars and planets

opulent: rich and luxurious

patron: someone who supports or protects a group or person

revered: deeply respected

rituals: religious or traditional ceremonies

sacrifices: acts of offering something to the gods – sacrificing, or killing, humans to please the gods was common in ancient Mayan society

sarcophagus: stone coffin, which is often richly decorated

scribes: people skilled in reading and writing Mayan glyphs

INDEX

ABOUT THE AUTHOR

I grew up in East Anglia, where my love of history was inspired by a history teacher who filled our heads with wonderful stories about the past. I studied history at the University of St Andrews and spent many years as a publisher of children's non-fiction books before becoming a writer. I would love to visit the ruins of the Mayan civilization with my wife and two sons.

Discovering the life and death of the Maya people has been fascinating. Even with all of the resources of modern science, experts still disagree about what happened to this fascinating civilization. Writing this book has convinced me that the fate of the Maya was caused by a mixture of different factors. I am fairly sure they were not abducted by aliens, but maybe that is what the aliens want me to think!

Greg Foot, Series Editor

I've loved science ever since the day I took my papier mâché volcano into school. I filled it with far too much baking powder, vinegar and red food colouring, and WHOOSH! I covered the classroom ceiling in red goo. Now I've got the best job in the world: I present TV shows for the BBC, answer kids' science questions on YouTube, and make huge explosions on stage at festivals!

Working on TreeTops inFact has been great fun. There are so many brilliant books, and guess what ... they're all packed full of awesome facts! What's your favourite?